Best wishes —

Margaret Carpenter

Seasons of Change

By Margaret Carpenter

Coleman Publishing
99 Milbar Boulevard
Farmingdale, New York 11735

Manufactured in the United States of America

ISBN 0-942494-60-1

Seasons of Change

By Margaret Carpenter

This book is a journey through seasons
of change as fall and winter, spring
and summer take on a deeper significance.
I invite you to share in the experience.

"The real voyage of discovery lies not
in seeking new lands, but in
seeing with new eyes."

Proust

CONTESSINA, forgive an old man's babble. But I am your friend and my love for you goes deep. There is nothing I can give you which you have not got; but there is much, very much, that while I cannot give it, you can take. No heaven can come to us unless our hearts find rest in it to-day. Take heaven. No peace lies in the future which is not hidden in this present little instant. Take peace!

The gloom of the world is but a shadow. Behind it, yet within our reach is joy. There is radiance and glory in the darkness, could we but see; and to see we have only to look. Contessina, I beseech you to look.

Life is so generous a giver, but we, judging its gifts by their covering, cast them away as ugly or heavy or hard. Remove the covering, and you will find beneath it a living splendour, woven of love, by wisdom, with power. Welcome it, grasp it, and you touch the angel's hand that brings it to you. Everything we call a trial, a sorrow, or a duty, believe me, that angel's hand is there; the gift is there, and the wonder of an overshadowing presence. Our joys, too; be not content with them as joys. They, too, conceal diviner gifts.

Life is so full of meaning and purpose, so full of beauty (beneath its covering) that you will find earth but cloaks your heaven. Courage, then, to claim it; that is all! But courage you have; and the knowledge that we are pilgrims together, wending through unknown country, home.

Letter written by a priest in 1513

As summer ends the young birches
are whipped by the winds of change;
but their roots are deep and their
trunks supple as they grow through
the seasons.

"Go forth, under the open sky, and list
to Nature's teachings."

Bryant

A still moment provides a
brief and graceful bridge
between the long summer days
and the coming of snow.

"Time out of mind......

Cervantes

Margaret
Carpenter

The contrasts of exploding color and
the soft September mist, the feel of
cool mornings and warm days.
These delight the senses.

"The tissue of the life to be
We weave with colors all our own."
Whittier

Light sparkles on the river and through the bright leaves, creating a drama in the late afternoon as the clouds move down the canyon from the west.

"There is nothing permanent except change."
Heraclitus

After the rain there is
a stillness that accentuates
the approaching moments
and colors of fall.

"Nature is a mutable cloud, which is
always and never the same."

Emerson

Margaret
Carpenter

The harmony of colors in
nature is revealed as clearly
in the bare bones of winter
as in the riot of summer.

"Nothing useless is, or low;
Each thing in its place is best."

Longfellow

Margaret
Carpenter

The pattern of tree trunks repeats
itself against the muted colors
of riverside brush in the subtle
light of a winter afternoon.

"The perception of beauty is a moral test."
Thoreau

There is the magic of classic ballet in
the soft colors of a misty winter's day.
The trees and branches bend and stretch
with the effects of time and season as
the snowflakes dance between them.

"Time is infinite movement....."

Tolstoi

Margaret
Carpenter

Familiar folds take on a glow,
and brief warmth is imparted
to a still, cold landscape.

"I have an understanding with the hills
At evening when the slanted radiance fills
Their hollows, and the great winds let them be,
And they are quiet and look down at me."

Conklin.

Were it not for the rocks
we would not see the beauty
of the spray; the exciting
interaction of land and sea.

"I must go down to the seas again..."
Masefield

For all the beauty of
wind and water, they are
a power to be reckoned with....
and respected.

"The sea never changes, and its works, for
all the talk of men, are wrapped in mystery"

Conrad

Margaret
Carpenter

There is a rare quality of light
on a sunny day at high altitudes
that enhances the incandescence of
the snow and brightens all perceptions.

"In the morning of the world
When earth was nigher heaven than now."

Browning

Margaret
Carpenter

Before the sap rises,
before the first buds open
on the willows, the robins
anticipate spring.

"And I sing a song as I go,
Of the blue, blue sky."

Tse Nan

Down by the pond, reflected
blue skies and signs of life
herald new beginnings in spite
of the March clouds.

"The gloom of the world is but a shadow"

Anon.

Margaret
Carpenter

Colors of dawn, elusive mists,
cries of hovering birds, sounds
of waves, and salt in the air....
all contribute to the new day.

"A heart awakened has eyes, perceives
the light in dark of night."

Angelus Silesius

Margaret
Carpenter

Delicate petals and fragrance of
apple blossoms provide transient
beauty against earth and sky, and
an assurance of fruit in its season.

"A thing of beauty is a joy forever
Its loveliness increases......"

Keats

Margaret Carpenter

Even though the flowers are
short-lived, the heady scent of lilacs,
carried on soft warm winds, brings joy
to the moment and promise of summer.

"For to-day, well lived, makes
Every yesterday a dream of happiness, and
Every to-morrow a vision of hope."

Sanskrit

What better on a summer's day than
to sit on a shady bank, lazily watching
the dragonflies dart among the willows
and skim lightly over the water?

"But life has such
Diversity, I sometimes remarkably lose
Eternity in the passing moment"

Fry

Early summer and water is high in the
lake as cottonwoods spring into life.
Sunlight and dappled shadows in the
reflections give rise to a restful mood.

"Nothing can bring you peace but yourself"
Emerson

Margaret
Carpenter

The grandeur and beauty of massive peaks, accessible only when the snow melts, is matched by the respect that the rugged terrain commands.

"We know the truth, not only by the reason, but by the heart."

Pascal

Margaret
Carpenter

Deep in the woods, there is something
very human about trees of every size
and configuration, existing together, —
rooted for survival and reaching for sunlight.

"And this our life, exempt from public haunt,
Finds tongues in trees, books in running brooks,
Sermons in stones, and good in everything."

Shakespeare

Margaret Carpenter

The hidden lake, soft swirling mists
and emerging peaks have such a
mystical beauty, that only the tangible
trees and ground can give them reality.

"There are truths which are not for all men
Nor for all times"

Voltaire

Margaret
Carpenter

Beauty can be as rare and fleeting as these poppies; but while they are in bloom they transform the barren field with such a blaze of flamboyant color that the memory of it lives forever.

"Someday, after mastering the wind, waves, tides and gravity, we shall harness.... the energies of love, and then, for the second time in the history of the world, man will discover fire."

Teilhard de Chardin

Photo by Nancy Rossman

BIOGRAPHY

Margaret Carpenter left her native England while still a young woman and has lived her adult life in the western United States. Artist, nurse, teacher, writer, wife and mother, she remains first, last and always an artist. She is an accomplished and talented watercolorist who knows what she is doing and why.

Her award-winning watercolors are hanging in collections in England, Hong Kong, California, Nevada, New York and throughout the Northwest where she had been painting for the past eight years. She has participated in juried shows in the Northwest and has had many successful one-woman shows. She is currently represented by galleries in Tahoe, Yakima and Seattle.

She has had a wide variety of arts experiences particularly in watercolor that has given her full command of this elusive medium. by combining her art with her background in nursing and teaching, Margaret also works with art therapy in a hospital setting and was recently featured on CBS "Newsbeat Magazine."

Within her landscapes there is strength, gentleness, reality and a special faith, a positive feeling that good has and will prevail despite hardship. Her work is neither contrived nor overly conceived. She paints what she sees and feels in an uncommon manner. Neither decorative nor abstract, she somehow wends her way between impression and expression, leaving the viewer to choose which road to take. Always leading, never demanding.

Lee Gwynne Mestres
Gwynne Galleries
Lake Tahoe

As with all creative endeavors, this book began with the smallest germ of an idea, and has grown out of many experiences. It is, in fact, the sharing of a journey through seasons of change, fall and winter to spring and summer. Because we are ever influenced, the experiences themselves, and our perceptions of them are subject to change, but there are continuities in the seasons and essential realities that never change.

This collection of paintings, observations and ideas is an expression of all that has brought me to this point in time. The people and circumstances that have become part of the fabric of my life; the traditional and innovative, the boundaries and freedoms, city life, farm life, travel and above all, the arts have contributed to and enriched "Seasons of Change."

The letter to "Contessina" came from a book that was written and compiled by my godfather and has been a favorite for many years. It is as relevant to-day as it was in 1513.

"I beseech you to look..."

Margaret Carpenter

Yakima, Washington
May 1983

Coleman Publishing
99 Milbar Boulevard
Farmingdale, New York 11735
(516) 293-0383-84